IT'S TIME TO EAT EARTHQUAKE COOKIES

It's Time to Eat EARTHQUAKE COOKIES

Walter the Educator

Silent King Books
A WhichHead Entertainment Imprint

Copyright © 2025 by Walter the Educator

All rights reserved. No part of this book may be reproduced in any manner whatsoever without written per- mission except in the case of brief quotations embodied in critical articles and reviews.

First Printing, 2024

Disclaimer

This book is a literary work; the story is not about specific persons, locations, situations, and/or circumstances unless mentioned in a historical context. Any resemblance to real persons, locations, situations, and/or circumstances is coincidental. This book is for entertainment and informational purposes only. The author and publisher offer this information without warranties expressed or implied. No matter the grounds, neither the author nor the publisher will be accountable for any losses, injuries, or other damages caused by the reader's use of this book. The use of this book acknowledges an understanding and acceptance of this disclaimer.

It's Time to Eat EARTHQUAKE COOKIES is a collectible early learning book by Walter the Educator suitable for all ages belonging to Walter the Educator's Time to Eat Book Series. Collect more books at WaltertheEducator.com

USE THE EXTRA SPACE TO TAKE NOTES AND DOCUMENT YOUR MEMORIES

EARTHQUAKE COOKIES

The cookies bake, the smell is sweet,

It's Time to Eat
Earthquake Cookies

A chocolatey, crackly treat!

Warm and soft, a joy to see,

Earthquake cookies, yum for me!

Look at them, oh, what a sight!

Cracks and crinkles left and right!

Baked with love, so fun to share,

A tasty treat beyond compare!

Sugar dusted, round and small,

Chocolate hiding in them all.

Take a bite and you will know,

A fudgy center steals the show!

Mix the batter, thick and bold,

Scoop and roll, don't let it fold!

Dip in sugar, make it neat,

Then they're ready for some heat!

It's Time to Eat Earthquake Cookies

Into the oven, now they go,

Watch them rise and crackle, whoa!

Little mountains, big and wide,

With chocolatey joy inside!

The timer dings, oh, what fun!

Earthquake cookies, baked and done!

Let them cool, but not too long,

That smell is simply much too strong!

One for me and one for you,

Take a bite, so soft and goo!

Warm and chewy, oh so sweet,

The best dessert you'll ever eat!

Milk and cookies, what a pair!

Dip and munch, no crumbs to spare!

Chocolate melts, so rich and deep,

It's Time to Eat
Earthquake Cookies

Earthquake cookies, dreams to keep!

Let's bake more, don't wait too late,

Shake and stir and fill your plate!

One, two, three, or maybe four,

I think I need just one bite more!

Share with friends and spread delight,

Cookies make the world so bright!

Big or small, they're fun to make,

It's Time to Eat
Earthquake Cookies

Hooray for cookies that earthquake!

ABOUT THE CREATOR

Walter the Educator is one of the pseudonyms for Walter Anderson. Formally educated in Chemistry, Business, and Education, he is an educator, an author, a diverse entrepreneur, and he is the son of a disabled war veteran. "Walter the Educator" shares his time between educating and creating. He holds interests and owns several creative projects that entertain, enlighten, enhance, and educate, hoping to inspire and motivate you. Follow, find new works, and stay up to date with Walter the Educator™

at WaltertheEducator.com

www.ingramcontent.com/pod-product-compliance
Lightning Source LLC
LaVergne TN
LVHW052012060526
838201LV00059B/3983